RAMSES II

THE MOST POWERFUL PHARAOH OF ANCIENT EGYPT

Leaders of the Ancient World™

RAMSES II

THE MOST POWERFUL PHARAOH OF ANCIENT EGYPT

Beatriz Santillian and
Susanna Thomas

Rosen YA™

New York

For Shamika, Frances, and Anita Davis —BS
For Joseph and Fred Thomas —ST

Published in 2018 by The Rosen Publishing Group, Inc.
29 East 21st Street, New York, NY 10010

First Edition

Library of Congress Cataloging-in-Publication Data

Names: Santillian, Beatriz, author. | Thomas, Susanna, 1966– author.
Title: Ramses II : the most powerful pharaoh of ancient Egypt / Beatriz Santillian and Susanna Thomas.
Description: First Edition. | New York : Rosen Publishing, 2018. | Series: Leaders of the ancient world | Includes bibliographical references and index. | Audience: Grades 7–12.
Identifiers: LCCN 2016053655 | ISBN 9781508174899 (library bound)
Subjects: LCSH: Ramses II, King of Egypt—Juvenile literature. | Pharaohs—Biography—Juvenile literature. | Egypt—Kings and rulers—Biography—Juvenile literature. | Egypt—History—Nineteenth dynasty, ca. 1320–1200 B.C.—Juvenile literature.
Classification: LCC DT88 .S25 2016 | DDC 932/.014092 [B] —dc23
LC record available at https://lccn.loc.gov/2016053655

Manufactured in China

On the cover: *Foreground*: One of the colossi of Ramses located in Luxor, Egypt. *Background*: Fresco from the great hall of Abu Simbel.

CONTENTS

INTRODUCTION

Contrary to ancient Egyptian tradition, the first ruler of the Nineteenth Dynasty was chosen not by hereditary succession but by the ruler at that time. Ramses I would successfully secure his authority so that when he died in 1295 BCE, his son Seti would expand his duties as co-regent to holding all the power of the throne. And later, Seti's son Ramses II would also follow a path of ascension that involved political maneuvering.

Outside of the theater of producing a royal family and placing members on the throne, there were many conflicts and duties that a pharaoh had to manage. Domestically, the pharaoh had to deal with questions concerning whether or not there was enough food for everyone and if it must be produced locally or imported. Wealth was a concern that impacted the people's

This fragment of wall painting shows people sowing and harvesting crops, a task that was likely delegated to enslaved people in ancient Egypt.

relationship to the ruling class, so power structures had to be in place to secure a labor force that wasn't wealthy enough to forego completing menial but abundant tasks by quitting or by rebelling—especially in a state that relied so heavily on slave labor.

There were international circumstances for the pharaoh to deal with, too. A nation ruled by a king inevitably had memories of struggles against competing settlements and constantly took part in military action. This usually manifested as the nation invading its competitor or being invaded. Trade or other peaceful interactions with another country could cause a change in the materials and even the values of the denizens, like when a stronger material for tools replaced what was domestically produced or when a polytheistic emperor claimed to be the descendent of a god from a different land.

While we follow the lives of kings and trace the evolution of a changing society, we must rely on artifacts to answer the questions that we create. There are many materials that are available for learning about the circumstances of ancient Egypt during the reign of Ramses II. Statues and burial sites are often accompanied by writings on the wall that tell of who is buried or depicted and what they accomplished. The government of ancient Egypt, in particular, kept official records of the actions and achievements of its kings, some of which they destroyed after Ahmose I deposed the Hyksos. And surviving records belonging to neighbors contest or corroborate the accounts of Egyptian records. Tools and items share a wealth of information about the material reality of the Egyptians, revealing information like how ancient Egyptian technological advancement compared with other groups and contrasts with the question of whether or not that had an impact on their ability to compete in economic and military arenas. Even bodies offer good evidence. If a mummy hasn't decomposed too much, the state of the body, including the presence of wounds and indications of health, could serve as confirmation of or a rebuke to the story that other evidence attempted to tell.

As we ask those artifacts questions, we must always interrogate the possibility that they don't always tell the truth. And we must scrutinize the myths that time and contemporary circumstances suggest if they have little evidence so that we recognize the limits of the study of history.

CHAPTER 1

ESTABLISHING THE THRONE

The end of the Eighteenth Dynasty meant the beginning of the reign of Ramses. And a new reign meant a new need to protect the image of royalty. That is what was at stake when an unexpected death welcomed a new Egyptian dynasty.

A NEW DYNASTY

Ramses II's grandfather, Ramses I, had been a general and a vizier under Horemheb, the last king of the Eighteenth Dynasty of ancient Egypt. He had held the title Deputy of the King of Upper and Lower Egypt, as had his friend and colleague Horemheb before him, and the transition of power seems to have been a peaceful one. Horemheb didn't have any children of his own to inherit the throne, and Ramses I must have seemed the safest and most sensible choice to be the next pharaoh of Egypt. His importance was reflected in the list of jobs he performed for Horemheb. These included Chief of Archers, Chief of Seals, Superintendent of Horses, King's Charioteer, Commander of the Army of the Ruler of Two Lands, High Priest of all the Gods, Superintendent of the Mouths of the Nile, and Hereditary Prince of the Entire Land.

Horemheb himself had not inherited the throne in the normal way, that is, by assuming it upon his father's death. He had been a successful general when his predecessor, King Ay, who also had no children of his own, appointed him to be the next pharaoh. The appointment of both these kings shows how important military positions were at this time. When Horemheb was in his sixties and Ramses I was in his fifties, Ramses I was appointed as the heir. Ramses's eldest son, Seti, was already an adult by this time and was a soldier who was married to Tuya, who also came from a military family. They had at least two daughters as well as a son, also called Ramses. This was an additional factor in Horemheb's decision to make Ramses I the successor. Ramses I had not only sons but grandsons to act as heirs to the throne and to carry on the new dynasty.

PREPARING FOR DEATH

Horemheb died in 1295 BCE, and the first royal act of Ramses I was to oversee his secret burial rites in the Valley of the Kings on the west bank of the Nile at Luxor. At the same time, Ramses I began preparations for his own tomb to be built near that of his friend Horemheb in the Valley of the Kings, as well as a memorial temple on the flood plain below the valley where ritual offerings could be made after he had died.

While still at Luxor, Ramses I decided to make his mark as the new ruler. The most important god in Egypt during the New Kingdom was Amen-Re, and the main center in the country for worshipping this god was at the Karnak Temple in Luxor. Ramses I and his son Seti planned to build a fabulous addition to this temple by adding a huge hall of enormous columns, called a hypostyle hall, in between the two existing pylon gateways. He also decided that the walls of the two gateways, as well as the ceilings and columns of the hall, should be

This diorite statue from the Luxor Temple in Egypt depicts Horemheb, the pharaoh who preceded Ramses I.

redecorated with pictures of temple rituals and the names of Ramses I and Seti.

After beginning these different building projects, Ramses I and Seti then sailed north down the Nile back to the capital at Memphis (near modern Cairo). Seti was sent back to the army, where he carried on his job of training troops, and he also lead a small military expedition into Canaan (modern-day Israel). Toward the end of the Eighteenth Dynasty, many of Egypt's territories in the Near East—Israel, Jordan, Lebanon, and Syria—had been lost, and one of Seti's main ambitions was to restore Egypt's Syrian empire. Ramses I also sent fresh supplies to a fortress at the other end of his empire in Nubia (modern-day Sudan) to reassure the troops posted there that they were not forgotten.

Unlike the kings of the Eighteenth Dynasty, whose families originally came from Luxor, Ramses I's family came from the northeast corner of the Nile Delta. Ramses I had a holiday house near Avaris where the Hyksos kings of the Second Intermediate Period had lived. Egyptians usually felt particular loyalty to the town or area where they were born, and it is likely that Ramses I planned

EGYPTIAN CO-REGENTS

From Dynasty XVIII up until the era of Ramses II, there were several co-regents, including Hatshepsut and Thutmosis III, possibly Amenhotep IV and Amenhotep III, Ankhkheperure Neferneferuaten, who served as Akhenaten's co-regent, Seti I, and Ramses, the prince regent.

The system of Egyptian co-regents was put in place to secure the ascendency of a later ruler. There were three circumstances in which the system of co-regents was used, thus creating the necessity for different power dynamics between them.

In one circumstance, a death had occurred. The designated successor of the throne would've been too young to ascend to power, so a more mature figure—often, a female member of the royalty—acted as a stand-in and as the main authoritative figure of Egypt until the designated heir was deemed old enough to fulfill the duties of the king.

The second circumstance is similar. When a ruler was becoming close to death, either because of age or illness, he might want to delegate at least some of the responsibilities to an heir who was considered old enough to rule.

The last circumstance was that establishing a co-regent could secure the smooth transition of power between one ruler to another, thus determining one

Scholars believe that Nefertiti (*right*) served as co-regent to Akhenaten (*left*) during the later portion of his reign.

designated heir out of a pool of many potentials. This type of co-regent might be a prince with many brothers, or a person who wasn't related to a royal family. And, this co-regent would share power with the king or queen, so that the original ruler was in control of deciding how much power to share.

to celebrate being made pharaoh by putting up special temples or palaces in this region. However, after about only one year in office, Ramses I became ill. He appointed his son Seti as co-regent, and after only one year and four months of ruling Egypt Ramses I died in 1295 BCE while living in Memphis.

PAYING RESPECTS TO THE DEAD

King Seti I was now in charge of the mummification and burial of his father. Unfortunately, the craftsmen in the Valley of the Kings had not had enough time to complete his tomb, and so, in the seventy days traditionally set aside for the embalming process, a much smaller version of the tomb for Ramses I was quickly finished off.

Seti I and his son Prince Ramses, who was now about eight or nine years old, sailed south from Memphis to Luxor accompanying the mummified body of Ramses I. People lined the banks of the river to watch both the passing of the old king and to catch a glimpse of their new ruler. On arrival at the west bank at Luxor, the dead king's body was taken off the royal barge, accompanied by the sounds of ritual prayers sung by the priests and loud wailing from women who were specially paid to act as professional mourners. A procession then led from the banks of the Nile to the memorial temple of Ramses I and then secretly on to the tomb of the king hidden in the Valley of the Kings. Here special rituals were performed by Seti and accompanying priests in front of the body of his father before the mummified figure was lowered into his coffin and the tomb was sealed.

After performing these rituals, Seti took the opportunity to pick out the site in the Valley of the Kings for his own tomb, and he ordered craftsmen to begin carving it out of the hillside. He also began the construction of his own memorial temple on the west bank. He and the child Ramses also visited the great temple to Amen at Karnak to check on the building work of the hypostyle hall. Seti now ordered that his name should be carved everywhere and that the hall should be called "Effective is Seti I in the domain of Amen." He also decided that the outsides of the

This image shows the facade of the Horus Temple, which is a hypostyle hall in Edfu, Egypt.

walls, which more people would see, should be covered in scenes of Seti I beating all his enemies in battle.

On the way back to Memphis, Seti and young Prince Ramses stopped off at Abydos, which was the center of the cult of Osiris, who was the most important god of the afterlife. Here Seti commissioned the construction of an unusual temple that would contain seven separate cult sanctuaries for the worship of all the important gods of Egypt. This building would also have a list of most of the previous kings of Egypt carved on its walls, and it is now famous for being the site of some of the most beautiful carvings from ancient Egypt. At the same time, Seti ordered the building of a smaller temple for his father, Ramses I, and a slightly larger one for his son, Prince Ramses. Back in the capital, Seti ordered improvements at the great temple to the god Ptah at Memphis and the temple of the sun god Re at Heliopolis. Seti's hometown was not forgotten, and in the eastern Delta he ordered the construction of a fine summer palace decorated with blue and white tiles.

SETI'S AMBITION

Now that Seti I was in charge, he was able to pursue his ambition of restoring Egypt's control of Canaan and Syria by beating all the local princes and chieftains who had taken the opportunity to rebel against Egypt toward the end of the Eighteenth Dynasty. Seti proclaimed that the tribal chiefs "have lapsed into confusion and quarrelling; each slays his fellow. They ignore the laws of the Palace."

Seti conducted a series of campaigns that are known as the Northern Wars. In year one of his reign (Egyptian years started over again at the beginning of each new king's reign) the Egyptian army marched from the northeast Delta across the Sinai desert as far as Gaza in the region of Canaan (in modern Israel). Here they fought an enormous battle with the local tribe who were called the Shasu. Seti then marched on as far as Beth Shan on the Jordan River, where he set up a stela to commemorate another victory. It reads, "His Majesty sent out the First Division of Amen, 'Rich in Bows,' against the town of Hammath; the First Division of Re, 'Abounding in Valor,' against the town of Beth

This is an image of the Beth Shan stela. The sun was a common ancient Egyptian symbol, representing Re. In this stela the sun is above Horus, the falcon deity.

Shan; and the First Division of Seth, 'Strong of Bows,' against the town of Yenoam. And so, when the span of a day had elapsed, they were all fallen to the might of his Majesty." In the next two years, Seti and his army returned again to Canaan and Syria and tried to finish the job of making peace and strengthening Egypt's hold on the region. His armies also secured for Egypt the coastal ports of Tyre, Sidon, Byblos, and Simyra.

The other great superpower at this time was the Hittite empire, which was based in Hatti (modern Turkey) in the north. This power also controlled territory spreading southward toward the Egyptian-controlled areas. King Seti and the Hittite king Muwatallis fought briefly in year four (1291 BCE). This was the beginning of a long series of conflicts between them.

CHAPTER 2

THE UPBRINGING OF RAMSES II

As a prince, Ramses II would be given many responsibilities to prepare him for his future role as king. This transitional period in his life saw him go from being the one who was too young to do anything to becoming, in decree and in action, the official heir to the throne.

THE YOUTH OF RAMSES II

Although by the age of ten Prince Ramses had been made "Crown Prince" and "Commander in Chief of the Army," he was actually left safely at home in Memphis during military campaigns.

He lived for most of the year with his mother, Tuya, and his sisters Tiya and Henutmire in the royal palace in the capital city of Memphis. The family went for holidays to their palace at Ghurob

This is an image of the mummy mask of Queen Tuya, Seti I's wife. She died c. 1259 BCE.

in the Faiyum. This location had been a favorite of the royal family since the Middle Kingdom and was famous for its beautiful gardens and lakes. Since the Eighteenth Dynasty, there had been a special palace here for the royal women, some of whom lived there all year round, and others, such as Queen Tuya, her daughters, and Prince Ramses's wives, who went for visits. The royal ladies ran a very lively and bustling palace compound, effectively a small town that was famous for making very fine linen used to make the royal family's clothes. Ramses enjoyed hunting fish and birds in the lake and the marshes. In the hot summer months the family also visited their palace at Avaris in the northeast Delta near the Mediterranean coast.

Prince Ramses went to school with other boys in the palace compound at Memphis to learn reading, writing, and mathematics. One of his teachers there was a man called Tia, who later on married Ramses's sister Tiya. The couple was eventually buried in a joint tomb that has recently been discovered at Saqqara. Sports were also an important part of a boy's education. Ramses learned how to use a bow and arrow and how to shoot targets while riding on a chariot. He also developed his strength by riding horses and wrestling with other boys.

Military training usually took place in special army camps, where soldiers learned how to drill and to use different weapons. Prince Ramses had his own special training but often visited these camps as part of his duties as commander in chief.

NEW RESPONSIBILITIES

In year four of Seti's reign, when Prince Ramses was thirteen, the opportunity arose for him to accompany the Egyptian army for the first time. While Seti was dealing with the Hittites in the north, Libyan raiding parties from the country to the west were causing trouble in the western Delta of Egypt. Seti hurried back to Egypt and, taking Ramses with him, conducted a brief but successful campaign to repel the Libyans and was proclaimed he "who overthrows those who rebel against him, who smites the tribes people and tramples down the Bedouin and the distant foreign lands of Libya, making great slaughter amongst them." Ramses almost certainly watched the battle from a distance, as his father would not have wanted to put

This particularly sunny shot of the Karnak Temple Complex in Luxor, Egypt, shows many pillars holding up the structure and the Obelisk of Queen Hapshetsut in the distance.

THE KARNAK TEMPLE COMPLEX

Karnak is an Egyptian city located near Thebes, on the east side of the Nile River. During the reign of Ramses II, the Karnak Temple Complex featured the temple, various gates and pylons, the hypostyle hall, the court, the sacred lake, and other features. Various structures in the complex are decorated with carvings that depict scenes from the lives of the pharaohs, including the peace treaty between Egypt and the Hittites, carvings of Seti I, and the Eighteenth Dynasty pharaoh Amenhotep IV. Since part of the temple was commissioned by Ramses II, it also has various statues of his image, and a good portion of the art depicts him and others who contributed to the construction of the temple of Karnak.

him in danger. But the prince is shown for the first time standing next to his father in the battle scenes carved on the walls at Karnak.

The next year Seti went back to Syria to continue his battle against King Muwatallis, and this time he took Ramses with him. The armies fought over an important city in northern Syria called Kadesh. Seti briefly won control of the city and erected a victory stela, most of which is now lost. However, Muwatallis fought back, and the two kings finally agreed to a truce where Egypt would keep all the coastal ports that Seti had previously won, but the Hittites would keep Kadesh. These battles, and the victory at Kadesh that soon turned to defeat, had a profound effect on young Prince Ramses. He never forgot that Kadesh had once been Egyptian and was determined that one day he would win it back once more.

Prince Ramses also accompanied his father in the course of performing royal duties inside Egypt. Together they went on regular inspections of the new buildings being put up in the important cities at Luxor, Abydos, and Memphis. Ramses also learned how to run the administration of the government and the civil service.

HEIR TO THE THRONE

During year seven, 1289 BCE, when Ramses was sixteen, Seti decided to announce to the whole country that Prince Ramses was definitely the heir to the throne and would one day be the next pharaoh. This was a sensible step. The Ramses family was still quite new to the throne, and Seti wanted to ensure that there would be no doubt in the minds of the army and the government that Ramses was an important person they should obey.

Consequently, an important ceremony was arranged where Ramses was crowned prince regent. The event is described by Ramses himself in an inscription on the wall of his father's temple at Abydos:

> It was Menmaatre [Seti] who brought me up. The Lord of All himself magnified me, while I was still a child, until I became ruler. He assigned me the land while I was yet in the egg. The officials paid homage to me when I was installed as Senior Prince . . .When my father appeared before the populace, I being

> just a youth in his embrace, he spoke thus concerning me, "Crown him as king that I may see his beauty while I yet live!" He had the Chamberlains summoned to set the crowns upon my brow . . . so he said of me, while he was yet on this earth, "He shall govern this land, he shall care for its boundaries, he shall give commands to the people." He spoke of me, his eyes filled with tears, so great was the love for me within him. He furnished me with a household from the Royal Harem, comparable with the beauties of the Palace. He selected for me wives throughout the land.

The royal titles of the pharaoh were made up of five "great names," which became his own on the day of his coronation. The particular identity and interests of the king were often reflected in the names selected. The last two names of the king, known as the prenomen and nomen, were enclosed in cartouches, that is, oval or oblong decorative frames. The prenomen was the king's formal name and was used for things like official statements and

This painted relief from the chapel of Osiris in Abydos, Egypt, depicts Seti I with Anubis.

foreign dealings. The nomen was the king's personal name and the one that was used by his family and friends. Ramses now had to choose what his five throne names would be.

The first three names he chose were "The Horus, Mighty Bull, Beloved of Maat," "He of Two Ladies, Conqueror of Foreign Lands," and "Horus of Gold, Rich in Years, Great in Victories." All of these show the emphasis that Ramses placed on his own and Egypt's military strength and power. Seti's last names were Menmaatre, "Enduring is the Maat of Re," and Seti-Meryptah, "Seti Beloved of Ptah." Ramses modeled his names on those of his father and called himself Usermaatre, "Strong is the Maat of Re," and Ramses-Meryamen, "Ramses Beloved of Re."

MARRIAGE TRADITIONS AND CEREMONIES

Ramses's home life now changed. His father had given him his own household with his own wives and concubines. This meant that he now moved from the main palace where his parents lived into another palace on the same grounds. Here, at the age of sixteen, he lived with his own servants, some of whom were childhood friends who had grown up with him in the palace compound. One of his best friends was Ameneminet, who was now appointed his personal companion. Another friend and servant was Menna, who was Ramses's shieldbearer, a sort of bodyguard. When Ramses rode in a chariot, Menna would go with him to protect him.

The wives provided for him were well-brought-up Egyptian girls from high-ranking families selected by Seti and his advisors as suitable partners for the future king. There were probably also some foreign girls who were the daughters of princes and chiefs from Canaan and Syria who wanted to please Seti. Unlike previous pharaohs, the first Ramses kings did not marry their own sisters. This was because Ramses I and Seti I did not actually come from a royal family, and to them the idea would have seemed rather peculiar. Ramses II, however, was later to marry at least four of his own daughters.

Ramses's two main wives were called Nefertari and Iset Nofret. We do not know very much about either of these women except that they were both about the same age as Ramses and were probably both from Egyptian families. Both girls were very fertile, and in a very short time Nefertari had a son called Amenhirwonmef, and then Iset Nofret had a son called Ramses. Nefertari then had another son called Prehirwonmef and a daughter called Bint-Anath, while Iset Nofret had another son called Khaemwaset. Other lesser wives in the royal household also bore Ramses children, and in the first ten years with his harem Ramses produced nearly forty children!

SHARING THE THRONE

Even though Ramses had now been declared joint king with his father, everyone understood that Seti was still the king and that Ramses was the deputy ruler who still did what his father told him to do.

The next few years saw Seti and Ramses concentrating on domestic affairs. Seti spent most of his time running the government of the country from Memphis. He and his wife Tuya went for holidays to his summer palace at Avaris in the northeast Delta. In the winter they went to Luxor, where they lived in palaces, now lost, near the main temple at Karnak and also on the west bank at his memorial temple at Gurna.

Ramses spent his time traveling up and down the country keeping an eye on all the building projects that had been commissioned by his father. As part of his training, he was sometimes trusted to lead royal missions on his own. In year nine, for example, when Ramses was eighteen years old, he was put in charge of an expedition to the granite quarries at Aswan, in the southern part of the country. This expedition was sent to mine a special kind of black granite that was used to make statues and obelisks to decorate the temples and palaces being built by Seti. One ancient record of this undertaking read:

> His Majesty commissioned a multitude of works, to make very great obelisks

> and great and marvelous statues in the name of His Majesty. He constructed great barges for transporting them, with ships' crews to match them, ferrying them from their quarry, with high officials and transport men hastening the work along. And his senior son (Ramses) was before them, doing good service for His Majesty.

Ramses was also thought to be experienced enough to lead the army on his own. In year thirteen, 1283 BCE, when Ramses was twenty-two, there was some unrest among the local population in northern Nubia. Ramses, along with his two sons, Amenhirwonmef (aged five) and Khaemwaset (aged four), went to Nubia and quickly subdued the unhappy Nubians. Scenes that Ramses later had carved on the walls of a small temple at Beit el Wali near the site of the battle show Ramses and his sons, each in their own chariot with a shieldbearer, charging against the enemy, who are shown running away. A Nubian women cries "We have never known such raging of a ruler, he is like Seth in the sky!"

This painted chest shows a pharaoh fighting Nubian warriors. Note the high-tech weapons of the Egyptians, and the minimal detail to that of the Nubian weaponry.

The next few years passed comparatively quietly. All the great building works progressed, and a few matters of unrest, including the appearance of pirates in the Mediterranean, were quickly dealt with. Ramses continued to learn from his father about all the duties associated with being ruler of Egypt. But in the summer of year sixteen, 1279 BCE, when Ramses was twenty-five years old, King Seti suddenly died while he and his wife Tuya were on holiday at his summer palace at Avaris.

CHAPTER 3

HIS NEW RESPONSIBILITIES

Ramses was now king. This was the moment that he had been trained for almost his whole life. He was in charge of a great country that stretched from the provinces of Nubia in the south to Canaan and Syria in the north, and he would have to maintain control of that territory. However, his first task was to oversee the burial of his father, King Seti.

THE JOURNEY TO THE FUNERAL

In August 1279 BCE, Ramses set off from Avaris with the embalmed body of his father, accompanied by his mother, his sisters, his major wives, and some of his children. They traveled in a group of boats or barges, which were the most common form of transport in a county where most movement happened on the river rather than by road. Boats were either sailed or powered by oarsmen or towed forward with ropes from the bank. Their first stop was at Heliopolis, which was the cult center of the sun god Re. Along with Amen, Re was the most important god during the New Kingdom. After saying prayers and making offerings to Re, the cortege then moved on to the capital at Memphis.

All the ships containing Ramses's family as well as the priests and important officials then set sail for Thebes. After Seti's body had been unloaded it was carried to his memorial temple at Gurna on the river plain on the west bank at Thebes. Here there was a big religious service that everyone attended. After this, a smaller group of just the most important priests and members of the family followed the coffin into the desert to the Valley of the Kings. They would have been followed by a long procession of people carrying all the things that would go into the tomb with the dead king. These included four canopic jars containing the parts of the king's body that had

This twentieth-century Christopher Klein lithograph speculates on the construction and design of the tomb of Seti I.

been removed during mummification. Each canopic jar had a lid representing one of the four sons of Horus, who were guardians of the entrails. Imset had a human head and guarded the liver, Hapy had a baboon head and guarded the lungs, Qebhsenuef had a falcon head and guarded the intestines, and Duamutef had a jackal head and guarded the stomach.

The technique of mummification developed throughout Egyptian history was, by the time of the New Kingdom, a very efficient way of preserving the body.

We still have good examples of preserved remains from this period. The body of Seti I has been badly damaged, but his head is remarkably well preserved and his mummy can be seen today in the Cairo Museum. Seti's tomb contained a huge granite sarcophagus that his coffin was lowered into. He also had a very beautiful inner sarcophagus made of alabaster and covered with carved scenes from the Book of Gates, colored with blue pigment. All the rooms and passages of the tomb were beautifully decorated with religious texts written in hieroglyphics and pictures of the king with various gods. Many objects were also put into the tomb in case the king needed them in his afterlife. These included furniture, clothes, food, jewelry, weapons, and books, as well as many objects of religious importance. Unfortunately his tomb was repeatedly robbed quite soon after he was buried, so we can only guess at the original splendor.

After all the objects had been placed in the tomb, Ramses and the high priests conducted the final religious ceremonies with the body and lowered Seti's coffin into place. The tomb was then closed and the door sealed.

TRADITIONS IN LIFE AND DEATH

Ramses also began planning his own memorial temple, which today is known as the Ramesseum. This was the main building from which the funerary cult of Ramses would operate after his death. In other words, it would be a large temple dedicated to the king and the location of offerings made by a large group of priests for his *ka*, or spirit, after he had died. His memorial temple would have a floor plan similar to other New Kingdom temples, but in this case there would also be a statue of Ramses in the inner sanctuary. The temple would actually form one part of a small town, all enclosed by a high mud brick wall. Other buildings included a palace for Ramses to stay in when he visited, a school for training religious and government scribes, a library, and many large granaries and warehouses where goods were stored.

On the east bank, the hypostyle hall at Karnak was still under construction, and Ramses changed the name once again to "Effective is Ramses II in Amen's Domain." He also decided to enlarge the

GRAVE ROBBING

Seti I's tomb was probably robbed by ancient Egyptians or people who were alive shortly after his death. But how do many museums come into possession of artifacts that were certainly created in a different country?

It often begins domestically, but it may also be the result of tourism or unethical excavations. Either way,

Discreet-looking tourists like these are often able to get away with stealing various types of relics.

there is a burglary. The thieves either sell or smuggle the stolen goods to a different country. Private collectors become involved in purchasing those goods, and then they sell them to museums.

If it happens through a series of thefts and unauthorized sales, then it is clearly illegal. But such activity often has no record.

When it is clear that an artifact was illegally purchased, a museum is often willing to return it. But that kind of clarity is hard to come by, considering how many artifacts may have been illegally acquired. And returning the artifacts requires the cooperation of museums that have previously complied in the illegal activity.

neighboring Luxor Temple by adding a new pylon gateway and a large open courtyard with columns around the edges. Ramses decreed that there would be a large statue of himself in between each column, as well as four large seated statues flanking the doorways. After ensuring that all these expensive and elaborate buildings were underway, in October 1279 BCE, Ramses and his family set sail northward back to the capital at Memphis.

This image shows the remains of the Ramesseum, the memorial to Ramses II located in Luxor, Egypt.

The next few years passed swiftly, with Ramses attending to the business of ruling the country. At some point, in year two of his reign (1278 BCE), he decided to alter his prenomen or throne name, which now became Usermaatre Setepenre, "Strong in Right is Re, Chosen by Re, Ramses Meryamen." He kept a close watch on the building projects in Memphis, Abydos, and Luxor. The king's dynamic activity is mirrored in the rather boastful inscriptions carved on the walls of his temples. In the Karnak Temple one inscription reads, "It was his majesty who gave the regulations and led the work on his monuments. All his plans came to pass immediately."

WATER LIKE GOLD

In theory, Ramses was in charge of every aspect of the government.

One of his main duties was to ensure the prosperity of the country. It should be noted that construction on such a massive scale was very expensive. The king's treasury had to support all the workmen involved in the building of the temples. Fortunately, the Egyptians had plenty of gold. Egypt was famous in the ancient world as a source of the precious metal, and about two hundred years before, the king of Mitanni had written to King Amenhotep III that, "In my brother's country [Egypt], gold is as plentiful as dirt."

The Egyptians obtained gold from the deserts to the east of the Nile Valley and also from Nubian deserts in the south. Mining and quarrying expeditions were carried out under military control, and in theory the king was the only person who was allowed to order the work. Many of the laborers were convicts, and being sent to the gold mines was often as bad as a death sentence, as working conditions were very difficult and dangerous.

Gold was usually extracted from veins running through the mineral quartz. Fires were lit inside the mines, which heated and cracked the face of the rock. Men then broke pieces off with hammers and picks. Lumps of rock were then carried outside the mine where they were first crushed by large stone mortars and then ground into a fine powder. This powder was then washed in water in flat pans so that the fragments of gold, heavier than the particles of rock, sank to the bottom of the pan. These fragments were then melted into small ingots.

Reports had reached Ramses that there was a rich source of gold at a particular spot in Nubia, but that it was almost impossible to work there. The reports said that, "there is much gold in the land of Akuyati, but the road is extremely difficult because of the water problem. Of the gold prospectors who went there, only half of them ever arrived there, for they died of thirst on the way along with the donkeys that went before them. There could not be found for them their needs for drinking, either going or coming back."

Ramses then summoned all his advisors to discuss the issue, stating proudly that, "I shall take the matter in hand." He sent a detailed list of instructions to the viceroy of Nubia for an ambitious well-building program, defying all past experience with the region, saying, "Water has never been struck in this territory since the time of the God, as you say. But I shall open up a well there

In this wall painting, metal workers are weighing and gathering ingots of gold.

yielding water daily." The construction program was obviously successful because a couple of months later the viceroy sent another letter that said, "Everything has happened just as your majesty said with his own mouth. Water appeared in the well at twelve cubits [eighteen feet] . . . Never has anything like it happened before. The chief of Akuyati rejoiced immensely. Those who were far off marveled and came to see the well created by the Ruler." The well was duly named "The Well of Ramses II, Valiant in Deeds."

CHAPTER 4

TAKING ON THE HITTITES

Like his father before him, Ramses II had his eye on Kadesh. The pursuit of conquering Kadesh would reveal some major shortcomings in his army's resources and in the army of his rival, Muwatallis.

REKINDLING AN OLD RIVALRY

In year four of his reign (1275 BCE), Ramses felt strong enough to turn to a problem that had rankled him since he was a boy. He had vivid memories of his father Seti's campaigns in Syria against Muwatallis, the emperor of the Hittites. In particular, he remembered the unsatisfactory stalemate reached at the city of Kadesh. Kadesh and the region of Amurru had been Egyptian territory since the reign of Tuthmosis III two hundred years earlier. These areas were lost during the reign of Akhenaten about one hundred years earlier. Ramses now decided to reconquer this region of modern-day Syria and perhaps even expand Egypt's empire into new territories to the north. He and his armies set off first for the coastal cities of Tyre and Byblos, which were already under Egyptian control, and from there he quickly overwhelmed the region of Amurru

This relief of the Battle of Kadesh can be found in the Ramesseum, Ramses II's memorial temple.

farther up the coast, though he did not reach the city of Kadesh, which was farther inland.

The ruler of Amurru, Prince Benteshina, was in theory a subject of the Hittite emperor, but he had no choice but to submit to Ramses and to declare that Amurru would now come under Egyptian control and pay taxes to Egypt instead. Ramses was not just fueled by romantic ideas of restoring the Egyptian empire. He was also motivated by the practical consideration of getting more money for the Egyptian treasury. However, Benteshina was afraid that Muwatallis would be furious with him, so he wrote a secret letter to the Hittite emperor saying that he had switched allegiance to Egypt but that he had been forced to do so and had no choice in the matter. Ramses and his armies set off back to Egypt to celebrate these victories and also to plan the next campaign against Kadesh and other cities farther inland.

Muwatallis was furious. He had received the letter from Benteshina and quickly realized that the young pharaoh Ramses was serious in his pursuit of northern territory. Muwatallis decided that Ramses needed to be taught a lesson. He vowed to the gods of Hatti that he would recover Amurru, stop the Egyptians from taking Kadesh, and chase Ramses all the way back to Egypt.

GATHERING FORCES

During the spring of 1274 BCE, Muwatallis assembled a massive army. Egyptian records suggest that the Hittites managed to gather together 2,500 chariots and 37,000 men. The royal scribes wrote:

> Now the vile foe from Hatti had come and brought together all the foreign lands as far as the end of the sea. The entire land of Hatti had come, that of Nahrin also, that of Arzawa and Dardany, that of Keshkesh, those of Masa, those of Pidasa, that of Irun, that of Karkisha, that of Luka, Kizzuwadna, Carcamesh, Ugarit, Kedy, the entire land of Nuges, Mushanet, and Kadesh. He had not spared a country from being brought, of all those distant lands, and their chiefs were there with him, each one with his infantry and chariots, a great number without equal. They

> covered the mountains and valleys and were like locusts in their multitude. He had left no silver in his land. He had stripped it of all its possessions and had given them to all the foreign countries in order to bring them with him to fight.

Ramses prepared his army at Piramesse in the eastern Delta. Archaeological evidence indicates that massive metal smelting works were established at the barracks in the city. From these, thousands of axes, arrowheads, spearheads, knives, and swords were hurriedly produced. We also know that chariots were manufactured here and that hundreds, if not thousands, of horses were stabled and trained here. Along with the weapons that had been in use since the Old Kingdom, which included spears, axes, and bows and arrows, there were a number of technical innovations in the New Kingdom. The horse-drawn chariot, first introduced by the Hyksos rulers of the Second Intermediate Period, was now the chosen conveyance of rich, young Egyptians. The king was also often shown on temple walls fighting from a chariot. Body armor made from small bronze plates sewn onto linen or leather jackets was also now in use, and a leather example was found in the tomb of Tutankhamen. Bows were now made from goat horn and bone glued to wood, and these were much more powerful and could shoot arrows much farther—more than 300 yards (274 meters)—than bows made from wood alone. A special dagger or sword with a curved blade called a *khepesh* was invented at this time.

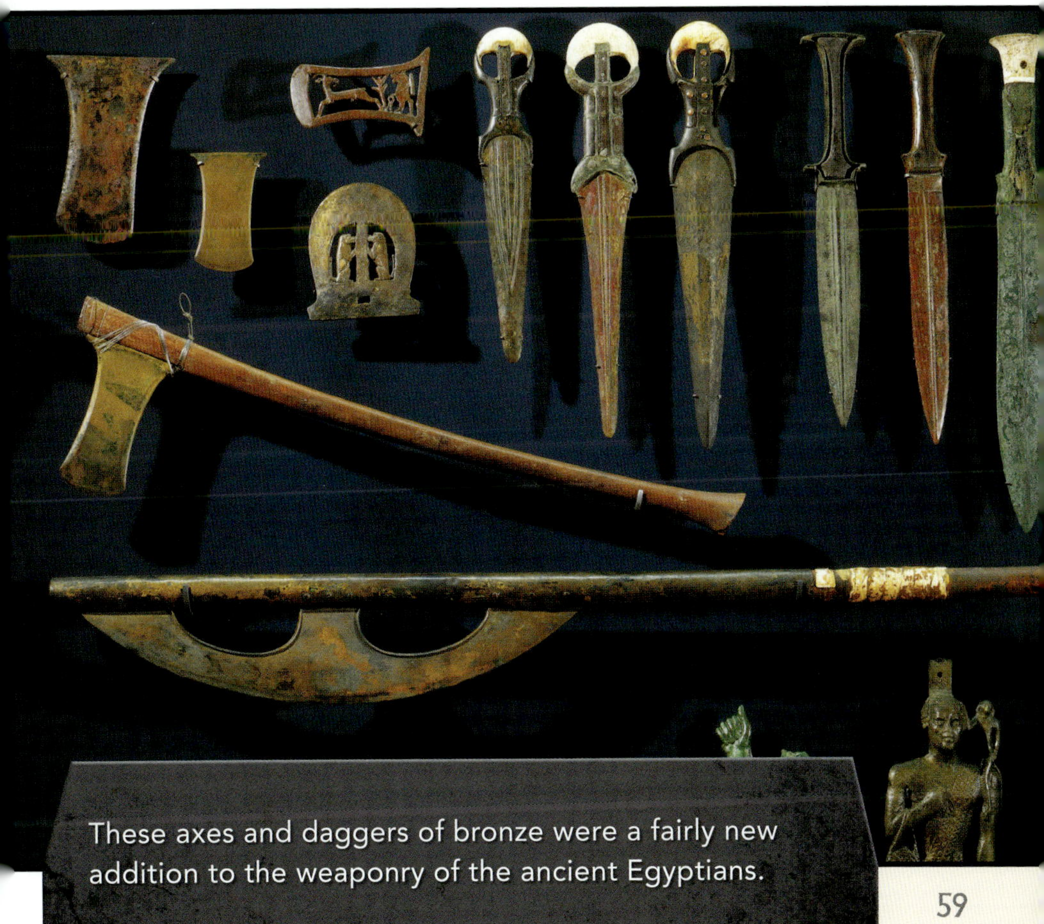

These axes and daggers of bronze were a fairly new addition to the weaponry of the ancient Egyptians.

PLOTTING THE COURSE

It was decided that Ramses and the bulk of the army would march overland from the eastern Delta toward Kadesh, while a supporting force would sail up the coast and march inland to meet up with the pharaoh. Ramses set off leading an army of twenty thousand men and chariots. The army was divided into four divisions of five thousand men each. These divisions were named Amen (probably made up of

RAMSES II'S ARMY

Way back in the time of Ahmose I of the Eighteenth Dynasty, the Egyptian army was restructured to have more modern weapons and training. Later, when it came to training and the overall structure of the military, Ramses II would enact his own reforms. He organized his domain into thirty-four nomes, or districts, and restructured the different types of fighting units into more manageable sizes. The redistricting allowed for smoother management, including more manageable conscription administration, training, and sending of supplies. Reorganizing the fighting units, specifically the chariotry and infantry, helped to more evenly distribute the talent of the fighters, and it helped with organizing the weapons of the infantry.

men from the Theban region), Re (from Heliopolis), Ptah (from Memphis), and Seth (from the eastern Delta). Ramses was also accompanied by one of the two viziers, some of his sons, his household staff, and his personal bodyguard. The troops and horses and chariots were accompanied by pack animals and ox-drawn carts carrying food, water, weapons, tents, and other necessary provisions. An account reads:

> His majesty journeyed northward, his infantry and chariots with him. He began the march well, in year five, the second month of summer, on day nine. His majesty passed the fortress of Sile [on the Egyptian side of the Sinai desert], being mighty like the god Montu when he appears, all foreign lands trembling before him, their chiefs bringing their gifts, and all rebels coming bowed down through fear of his majesty's might.

After a month's travel, the army reached Kumidi. Then Ramses and his household troops

This illustration shows Ramses II (notably larger than everyone else) attacking his Hittite rivals.

and personal bodyguard and the division of Amen set off northward toward the Orontes River, which they had to cross in order to reach the city of Kadesh. The other three divisions followed behind, and the army stretched back for many miles. As they marched through the woods of Labwi, two Bedouin tribesmen were found hiding in the trees. They said that they were deserters from the Hittite army and had come to fight for Ramses. "We will be servants of Pharaoh and will abandon the chief of Hatti." They also told the king that the massive

Hittite army was 120 miles (193 kilometers) farther north. "The foe from Hatti is in the land of Aleppo to the north of Tunip. He was too fearful of Pharaoh to come southward when he heard that the Pharaoh had come northward." Ramses and his advisers were pleased by this news because it indicated that they would be able to conquer Kadesh without much opposition. They and the Amen division crossed the river, rode north toward the city, and began to set up camp on the plain to the west.

A FAILED STRATEGY

However, as Ramses set up camp with the Amen division, and as the Re division marched up the plain toward the camp, and as the Ptah and Seth divisions prepared to ford the river to the south, disaster struck. The army had been lulled into a false sense of security by the information from the captured Bedouins that the Hittite army was still many days' travel away. Scouts sent out from Ramses's camp now captured two Hittite spies near the city of Kadesh, and they were brought before the pharaoh, though probably tortured first. "His majesty said to them 'What are you?' They replied 'We belong to the ruler of Hatti. He sent us to see where your Majesty was.' His majesty said to them 'Where is he, the Foe from Hatti? I have heard that he is in the land of Aleppo north of Tunip.' They replied, 'Behold, the Ruler of Hatti has already come, together with the many foreign lands that he brought as allies . . . They are equipped with their

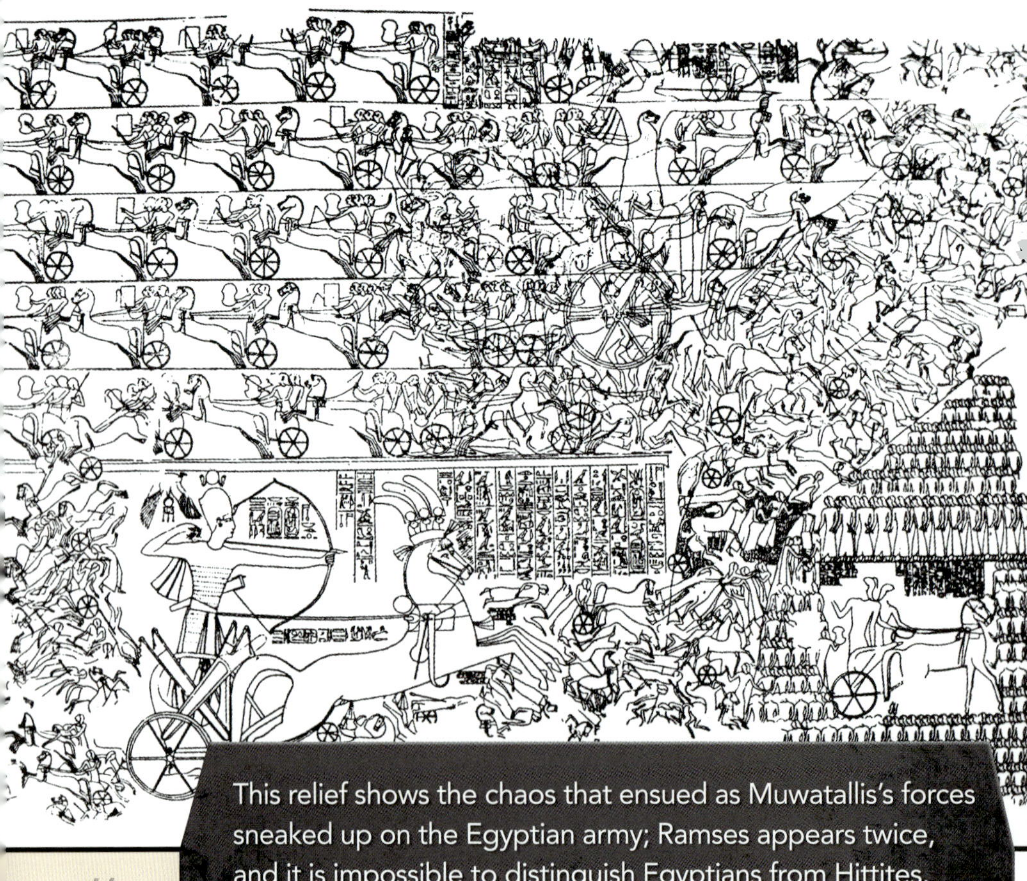

This relief shows the chaos that ensued as Muwatallis's forces sneaked up on the Egyptian army; Ramses appears twice, and it is impossible to distinguish Egyptians from Hittites.

infantry and their chariots and their weapons of war. They are more numerous than the grains of sand on the beach. See, they are poised armed and ready to fight behind Kadesh!'"

This was a disaster! The Hittite army was not 120 miles away but could attack at any moment. Ramses was furious at the uselessness of his intelligence services and immediately summoned his chief officers to tell them the appalling news. "See what state my provincial governors and high officers are in, that they go round saying daily 'Oh, the Hittite ruler is in Aleppo, away north of Tunip!' But now, this very hour, have I heard from these two Hittite spies, that the Hittite ruler has already come with his allies, his innumerable troops. Even now they are poised hidden behind Kadesh, and the generals and officers in charge of my territories were unable to tell us that they had come!"

CHAPTER 5

EGYPT AND ITS NEIGHBORS

Even in the middle of the most dangerous battle of his life, Ramses's ambition would remain unrelenting. That persistence in seeking new battles would eventually land him in the midst of rebels and refugees, two very different situations that needed the attention of a strong ruler.

FIRST BLOOD

In the camp of the Amen division countermeasures were taken as quickly as possible. The vizier was sent galloping off to the Ptah and Seth divisions to tell them to hurry across the river, while the royal family, who had accompanied the king to the site of the battle, fled westward out of danger under the leadership of Prince Prehirwonmef.

All of these hasty preparations were observed by the Hittite army under the command of Muwatallis. His army was concealed on the east bank of the river opposite the city. They had seen the Egyptian king and the Amen division arrive at the site. They could also see the Re division straggling across the plain. The sight of the vizier galloping south was probably just the sign they were waiting for. Suddenly a massive force of chariots, led by several Hittite princes, dashed westward across the river south of the city and headed toward the Egyptian army, still partly strung out along its line of march. The Re division was taken by complete surprise. The soldiers forgot all their military training in the panic, and instead of fighting back they scattered and fled north, leading the enemy right into the Egyptian camp. Seeing the distraught soldiers and the huge dust cloud of enemy chariots heading toward them, many of the Amen division also lost their heads and rushed around in confusion. The Hittite chariots swept around the camp and burst through the defensive line of shields along the western side of the camp. All seemed lost. His army was being wiped out around him, and at any moment Ramses could be captured or killed.

THE LONE WARRIOR

Ramses threw on his armor and leapt onto his chariot. In vain he tried to rally his panicked troops, but he was ready to fight to the death. He later told his version of the events that followed:

> When Menna my shieldbearer saw that a large number of chariots surrounded me, he became weak and faint-hearted, great fear invading his body. He cried out to his majesty "My good lord, mighty prince, we stand alone in the midst of battle, abandoned by soldiers and chariots, why do you stay to save them? Let us get clear, save us Usermaatre Setepenre!" His majesty said to his shieldbearer "Stand firm, steady yourself, my shieldbearer! I shall go for them like the pounce of a falcon, killing, slaughtering, and felling them to the ground." His majesty then rushed forward, at a gallop he charged into the midst of the foe. I was after them like Baal [the Syrian war god]

> in his moment of power, I slew them without pause.

So Ramses managed to stay alive and hold off the Hittite attack while his troops were panicking all around him. It is not clear how long he would have managed on his own, but help soon arrived. The division of soldiers who had sailed to the Syrian coast and marched eastward inland to join up with the royal army suddenly appeared on the scene. They immediately began to attack the Hittite charioteers. The Hittites now found themselves caught between a furious Ramses and a brand new army arriving from the west. These extra troops came as a complete surprise to the Hittites, whose military spies were obviously not much better than the Egyptian ones.

Together, Ramses and the new division managed to push the Hittites away from the camp. The Hittites, now wondering if any more Egyptian divisions were about to appear, suddenly turned and fled back toward the river and the main Hittite camp to the east. Muwatallis had stayed behind at the Hittite camp, and as he heard the sounds of battle in the distance he probably imagined that the

A BRIEF HISTORY OF THE CHARIOT IN ANCIENT EGYPT

It is believed that the place known as the Kazakh steppe in central Asia is where the chariot was invented approximately 3500 years ago. Toward the middle of the first millennium BCE and after the time of Ramses II, Sun Tzu wrote of four horses pulling a single chariot, so some of them must have been heavy.

The mysterious Hyksos peoples were the ones who introduced the chariot—and the horse—to the Egyptians during the time of the Seventeenth Dynasty (1580–1550 BCE). But the chariots of Ramses II would have been faster than his Hittite enemies' and were carried under the power of only two horses.

This photo shows a model of an Egyptian chariot that was likely used c. 1500 BCE. A light vehicle like this was good for carrying archers.

Egyptians were being soundly beaten. He must have been very shocked to see the Hittite chariots being chased into the river by Egyptian troops with the Pharaoh leading them. Before Muwatallis's horrified gaze, the Hittite army struggled into the water, with princes and soldiers alike swimming for their lives. A scene on the walls of the Ramesseum even shows that Rebeyer, the prince of Aleppo, swallowed so much river water on the way across that his retainers had to hold him upside down by the ankles to empty him out.

As the Hittites struggled back to their camp, the Ptah division finally arrived, led by the vizier, and the stragglers and disorganized elements from the Amen and Re divisions slipped back into the Egyptian camp. The Seth division finally arrived later that night.

MUWATALLIS'S LOSSES

Both rulers spent the evening assessing the damage to their armies. The Amen and Re divisions had suffered many casualties, but the Ptah and Seth divisions were still intact, as well as the bulk of the support force. The two Hittite infantry divisions, more than thirty thousand troops altogether, were unharmed, but the chariot division had suffered many losses. Sadly for Muwatallis, many of his army leaders had been killed in battle or drowned, and the losses included two of the emperor's brothers, two of his shieldbearers, his secretary, and the chief of his bodyguard.

The two largest armies ever seen now faced each other across the Orontes River. Large-scale open battle between rival armies was not the normal type of warfare during this period. The Egyptians were used to overpowering smaller states one at a time, while the Hittites preferred to ambush their enemies. Nevertheless, early the next morning Ramses attacked the Hittite camp in force. Without chariots the Hittites could not push the Egyptians back, but Muwatallis's army was much larger than Ramses's, and they stood their ground. No one could win this battle, and the Egyptian army finally disengaged.

As he had done fifteen years before with Seti I, Muwatallis now sent a letter containing peace proposals to the Egyptian camp. It concluded "Peace is better than fighting. Give us breath!" Ramses summoned another meeting of his chief officers and read them the letter. A truce was finally agreed upon, and Ramses and his armies returned to Egypt to celebrate the "victory." Ramses was so proud of this campaign that he had versions of the story carved on the walls of many temples in Egypt, including the temples at Karnak, Luxor, the Ramesseum, Abydos, and Abu Simbel. It is worth remembering, however, that he didn't actually achieve what he had set out to. Kadesh was not conquered or captured, and Amurru fell back under Hittite control. Poor Prince Benteshina was deposed from the throne and sent into exile in Hatti, where he ended up as the servant to the emperor's brother Hattusil. As for Muwatallis, he had stopped the Egyptians from expanding northward, but he had also lost many close friends. Also, Adadnirari I, the king of Assyria, had taken the opportunity to steal a piece of the Hittite empire called Hanigalbat while the Hittites were occupied with the Egyptians.

REBELLION AND INVASION

During 1273 BCE, Ramses concentrated on rebuilding his army at home. However, many of the Egyptian subjects in Caanan and Syria took this as a sign of weakness and began to disobey Egyptian orders. They stopped paying taxes. In the spring of 1272 BCE, Ramses once more turned his attentions to the north. He marched to Gaza and swiftly beat off marauding bands of Bedouin tribesmen who had been causing unrest. His eldest son, Prince Amenhirwonmef, who had now changed his name to Amenhirkhopshef, led another army north, and between them they reasserted Egyptian power in Canaan. The next year (1271 BCE) Ramses led the army north again. He advanced as far as Tunip, but he avoided Amurru and the city of Kadesh. He left a statue of himself in the main temple at the city of Dapur and then returned to Egypt in triumph.

Why had the Hittites not responded to this second provocative invasion? The reason was that after many years on the Hittite throne, Muwatallis had died. He was succeeded by his unpopular son, Uri-Teshub, who ruled as Mursill III, and who was busy at home in a political struggle with his powerful uncle, Hattusil. Nevertheless Tunip returned to Hittite rule as soon as Ramses had left, and in year ten (1269 BCE) Ramses returned to Dapur once more. These yearly campaigns continued until the situation was finally resolved in year twenty-one.

THE DIVINE NUBIAN RULER

Ramses now turned his attention to Nubia in the south. He had ordered the construction of two temples to be carved into a hillside on the west bank of the Nile a few miles south of Aksha. One was to have four colossal statues of the king carved out of the rockface, and the other was dedicated to the goddess Hathor and the king's wife Nefertari. The front of this temple was to be decorated with alternating statues of the king and queen. An old friend called Ashahebsed was dispatched to control affairs in Nubia and oversee the work on the temples.

Between the years ten and eighteen there are few documents that tell us exactly what the king was doing. Although the temples built by Ramses II are covered with scenes of wars with enemies both north and south, it is not always easy to tell exactly what is happening. It is clear that at some time around the year twenty some of the Nubians rebelled and tried to get rid of their Egyptian rulers. Ramses sent an army led by his sons Setemwia and Merenptah to help the viceroy of Nubia. Egypt quickly defeated the

This 1845 illustration depicts the Temple of Gerf Hussein, one of the temples Ramses II had constructed after suppressing a Nubian rebellion.

rebels, and seven thousand captives were taken back to Egypt. To celebrate the victory, a new city was built at Amara called "Ramses the Town." Ramses now ordered the construction of a number of temples in Nubia at Beit el-Wali, Gerf Hussein, Wadi el-Sebua, and Ed-Derr.

In Egypt, Ramses was viewed by his people as a human king who was also a kind of god as the son of Osiris and the representative of Horus on earth. In Nubia, however, Ramses was portrayed as a true god. The Nubians were a conquered people firmly under the control of the Egyptian state, and it was to be expected in this situation that the dominant power would use frightening and overwhelming images to reinforce fear of the victor's power. Massive statues of the king as god were carved to strike fear and obedience into the local population, with any religious significance a secondary consideration. It is also clear, because of the way that Ramses was increasingly portrayed as a god in temples built later in his reign, that the notion of his own divinity was taking hold throughout Egypt and its territories.

RAMSES REACTS TO LIBYAN REFUGEES

Trouble was also brewing on the western edge of Egypt's empire. At the beginning of the reign of Ramses II traditional Libyan tactics—small warrior bands making lightning strikes into the Nile Valley—had caused only minor difficulties for the Egyptians. Now Libya had suffered a long period of drought, and whole populations of nomadic clans were marching east across the desert toward the Egyptian Nile Delta. These groups were made up of men, women, and children with all their worldly possessions, including herds of goat and cattle. Another group called the sea peoples, who were made up of refugees from wars in Greece and Sardinia, as well as various pirates, were also looking for new places to live and threatening the Mediterranean coast from the sea.

Ramses decided that drastic action was needed. He set up a chain of fortresses stretching north from Memphis up along the western edge of the Delta to the sea, and then out west along the coast toward Libya. The farthest of these fortresses

In drought, many permanent homes are abandoned as people join nomadic clans seeking food and water.

was sited at Zawiyet Umm el-Rakham, which is about 185 miles (300 km) west of Alexandria.

This fortress was situated at least one week's march from the edge of the western desert. It had square walls 500 feet (150 m) long, 16 feet (5 m) wide, and over 32 feet (10 m) high, and one entrance on the north side was protected by limestone towers.

This illustration depicts an attack on an Egyptian fortress. It is unclear who the assailants are.

The walls enclosed what was effectively a small town, with temples, the palace of the commander (called Neb-Re), rows of storerooms, wells for fresh water, a village of small houses for the soldiers, workshops for making and mending weapons, kilns for making pottery, stables, and a chariot park. Other goods such as olive oil, wine, and opium imported from Crete, Greece, Cyprus, and Syria show that the fort was also a center for trade with merchants who sailed south from Crete. However, the fortress would have been an unpleasant and frightening place to stay, as it was in the middle of nowhere and

was called "the ends of the earth" by the Egyptians, as well as surrounded by unfriendly Libyan tribesmen.

The other fortresses on the Mediterranean coast were probably similar in size. Some existing towns along the western edge of the Delta were now also turned into fortresses. Excavations at sites such as Tell Abqa'in have shown that these settlements were enclosed with the same high, thick, mud brick walls. Ramses made his mark at all these sites. In addition to covering the temple walls with paintings of himself, he even had his name carved on the inside of the new limestone wells constructed to give fresh water to the inhabitants.

CHAPTER 6

ENDINGS

To the end of his life, Ramses II would successfully fulfill his duties as the king. It would seem that he knew that he couldn't go on for much longer because of his shift from militaristic action to working toward peace. The lengthy amount of time that he lived may have also indicated to him that he should prepare for the conclusion of his reign and for the transition of power to one of his sons.

BUILDING UP EGYPT

Construction was continuing in other cities throughout Egypt. The new capital city at Piramesse was taking shape. Large temples, to Amen, Re, Ptah, and Seth, were built at the four corners of the city. The original summer palace of Seti stood in the center of the town, and Ramses greatly enlarged this building, adding large halls, reception rooms, bedroom suites, and gardens. He also built a vast hall in which to celebrate his first jubilee in year thirty (1249 BCE). Many noblemen and government officials had large villas in the new city, and it was also home to many thousands of craftsmen, soldiers, and traders. The city soon became known throughout Egypt and beyond for the beauty of the new buildings. A letter from the scribe Pebes to his master Amenemope describes the new city.

> I have arrived at Piramesse, Beloved of Amen, and found it in extremely good condition . . . The residence is pleasant to live in; its countryside is full of everything good, and it has food and drink every day.

At Memphis, Ramses added halls to the main Ptah Temple and erected a series of colossal statues

This is an overhead shot of Qantir, which is thought to be the location of Piramesse.

of himself that lined the entrance way to the southern gate. He later boasted about this on a large stele erected in his temple at Abu Simbel, where it was written: "I have enlarged thy house at Memphis, protected with everlasting works, with excellent labor, in stone wrought with fold and genuine costly stones."

At Thebes the hypostyle hall at the Karnak Temple was finally finished and decorated. Ramses ordered that it should be opened for public worship, and he called it "The Place Where the Common People Extol the

The pylon gateway at the Luxor Temple has survived in much better condition than other ancient construction projects.

Name of His Majesty." The pylon gateway and courtyard at the Luxor Temple were also finished, and thirteen colossal statues of the king now stood in the new courtyard. There were also two seated and four standing statues of the king in front of the temple where everyone could see them. Passersby would have prayed to these and other statues of the king so that he might speak to the gods inside the temples on their behalf.

Work also continued on his memorial temple, the Ramesseum, on the west bank of the Nile. This temple was a mixture of traditional and new features. The most noticeable innovation was an enormous seated statue of the king in the first court, which is estimated to have weighed 1,000 tons (907 tonnes). Inside the temple, the walls were decorated with traditional themes of the king and the gods, as well as matching processions of his sons and daughters marching across the walls.

THE TREATY

After seven years on the Hittite throne, Mursill III was deposed by his more popular uncle Hattusil. Now called Uri-Teshub, Mursill was sent into exile in Syria. Here he tried to stir up a rebellion against

Written on this terracotta slab are the terms of the Egyptian-Hittite peace treaty.

his uncle and was promptly banished to Cyprus. From there he escaped to Egypt and the protection of Ramses II, where he continued his campaign against Hattusil.

However, unfortunately for Uri-Teshub, Hattusil was a very good negotiator. He sent a diplomat to Egypt carrying a letter from the emperor of the Hittites to the pharaoh of Egypt. After many years of fighting, a peace treaty was finally agreed upon between them. This treaty was engraved in a script called cuneiform on two huge silver tablets. Excerpts from this treaty were also carved onto the walls of the Karnak Temple and the Ramesseum, and they are also to be found on a clay tablet from the Hittite capital at Hattusas. The treaty included many interesting provisions in addition to a formal declaration of peace. The two kings agreed to stop fighting over Syrian territory and to form a defensive alliance against the Syrians. Political refugees and immigrants living across the border were extradited to their native countries. An interesting provision at the end of the treaty outlines the humane treatment to be shown to the people affected by the extradition clauses: "Let not his house be injured, nor his wives, nor his children, let him not be killed, and let no injury be done to his ears, to his eyes, to his mouth, nor to his feet."

Both sides now celebrated the peace. Hattusil sent greetings to Ramses, and his wife Pudukhepa wrote to Queen Nefertari, and she wrote back, "With me your sister, all goes well; with my country all goes well. With you my sister, may all go well, with your country may all go well." After more good wishes, she ends the letter, "Now I am in friendship and sisterly relations with my sister, the Great Queen, now and forever."

Friendship grew between the two countries. Correspondence continued between the two rulers. They sent each other many presents, including objects of gold and jewelry. The Egyptians, famous for their medical knowledge, also sent doctors to the Hittite royal family. In year thirty-three (1246 BCE) Hattusil offered to send his daughter to marry Ramses. This marked the end of the wars of Ramses II, and for the rest of his reign Egypt was generally at peace with its neighbors.

RAMSES II'S FAMILY

Queen Nefertari was Ramses's favorite wife. She had at least ten children with him, including his eldest son Amenhirwonmef, his third son Prehirwonmef, and one of his favorite daughters, called Meryetamen. His smaller temple at Abu Simbel was dedicated in part to Nefertari, and she and Meryetamen traveled with the king to the opening of the great temples at Abu Simbel in year twenty-four (1255 BCE). She seems to have died soon after and was buried in the Valley of the Queens on the west bank of the Nile at Thebes, where her tomb is one of the most beautiful in Egypt.

Iset Nofret now became the principal queen, but she also seems to have died soon after, although her tomb has not yet been found. Ramses now needed a new queen. The most suitable wife for a king of Egypt was the daughter of a king of Egypt, and so Ramses married his own daughter, Bint-Anath. He was later to marry two other daughters, Meryetamen and Nebettawi, and his sister Henutmire.

Bint-Anath and Meryetamen shared the role of chief queen until year thirty-four, when they were joined by the Hittite princess. In autumn 1246 BCE, the eldest daughter of Hattusil and

AN EGYPTIAN TRADITION

From the time of the earliest kings of Egypt, a special ritual had been performed to renew the king's powers. This was called the *heb-sed*, or jubilee festival. In the New Kingdom, the first heb-sed was performed in the thirtieth year of the king's reign and then every three years afterward. In year thirty, 1250 BCE, Ramses's first jubilee was organized by Prince Khaemwaset in the specially built hall at Piramesse. This massive celebration lasted for two months, with all the high officials presented to the king and with many ceremonies where the king was recrowned with the crowns of Upper and Lower Egypt. Religious services also took place in all the other temples in Egypt, and it was a time of mass celebration throughout the country. Because Ramses reigned for so long, he went on to celebrate thirteen more jubilee festivals.

Pudukhepa left the castle in the Hittite capital at Hattusas and traveled through Syria, Canaan, and the Sinai toward Egypt. She was accompanied by presents of animals, slaves, and precious jewels. Her mother came with her as far as Kadesh, where the group was met by Egyptian officials. Finally, in February 1245 BCE, she arrived at Piramesse to be welcomed by Ramses II. The whole county erupted in official celebration (paid for by the king), and a description of the marriage was carved on stele in temples throughout Egypt. Ramses named his queen Maathoreneferure, meaning "She who sees the Falcon (Ramses) who is the visible splendor of Re." She lived in the royal palace for a while and is written about in various inscriptions. However, her attraction seems to have paled quite quickly, and she was eventually sent off to live in the harem palace at Ghurob in the Faiyum.

Ten years later another Hittite princess was sent to marry Ramses, but sadly we know neither her name nor what became of her.

Ramses had as many as one hundred children. He outlived many of them, and between years twenty and thirty many of his sons died, including Amenhirkhopshef and Prehirwonmef. Ramses III was next heir to the throne, but he too died sometime between years twenty-five and fifty. The next heir was Prince Khaemwaset, an important priest at Memphis. The fifth heir was Ramses's thirteenth son, Merenptah, and it was he who eventually succeeded Ramses on the throne.

THE END OF RAMSES II

The latter part of Ramses's reign passed without major incident. He was still active in his fifties and sixties, but he had outlived all of his friends and many of his wives and children and was probably rather lonely in his later years.

In year sixty-six of his reign, at the age of eighty-nine or ninety, Ramses celebrated his fourteenth jubilee. He passed that winter in his palaces at Piramesse and Memphis. Medical evidence from his body shows that he suffered severe arthritis in his hips and hardening of the arteries in his lower legs, which would have made walking

These chapels in the jubilee court located in Saqqara, Egypt, served as the place were jubilee celebrations occured.

very painful. His teeth and gums were also badly decayed, probably causing constant toothaches.

In the spring and summer of 1213 BCE, Ramses stayed in his palace at Piramesse. Finally, in August of 1213 BCE, Ramses died. During the next seventy days his body was carefully embalmed, and the new pharaoh Merenptah and his entourage accompanied the king's body as it sailed slowly up the river to Thebes. They disembarked on the west bank, and after conducting religious services in his temple, the Ramesseum, Ramses II was carried to the Valley of the Kings, where his body was finally laid to rest in his tomb.

Ramses II is a major figure in Egyptian history. He restored Egypt's power and glory throughout the ancient world, thereby completing what his grandfather and father had set out to do. He promoted many able men to run Egypt's vast bureaucratic government system, and he added many beautiful buildings to Egypt's cities. Indeed, Ramses built or added to more temples throughout Egypt and Nubia than any other pharaoh. His memory lived on throughout Egyptian history, and for the next one thousand years he and his colossal statues were worshipped. Even today, his name and image live on, and he is remembered as Ramses the Great.

cubit The main Egyptian unit of measurement, approximately the length of a man's forearm that was divided into seven palm widths, each four thumb widths (or digits) wide.

dynasty A system of rule in which rulers come to the throne by hereditary descent. The reason for the change from one Egyptian dynasty to the next is not always clear, but it is usually associated with a change in the royal family or the location of the capital.

fortress A place that has been set up so that an army can easily defend it by protecting it with walls, armor, and troops.

heb-sed The ritual of royal regeneration, usually celebrated after thirty years of the king's reign but occasionally performed earlier. After the first time, this ritual occured every three years.

Hittite The name given to people of the Hittite empire, which was based in Hatti (modern-day Turkey).

jubilee The heb-sed festival.

ka The life force of every ancient Egyptian.

Libya The land west of the Nile River; Libyans are people from that land.

Lower Egypt The northern half of the country, stretching from Memphis to the Mediterranean coast.

Maat A goddess who embodied aspects of truth, justice, and harmony in the universe and whose power regulated the seasons and the movement of the sun, the moon, and the stars.

memorial temple A temple where the mortuary cult of the king was celebrated.

Memphis Known as Ineb-hedj or "White Walls," capital city of ancient Egypt that was the cult center of the god Ptah.

nomes Name used in the Ptolemaic period for the forty-two districts or provinces that Egypt was divided into.

Nubia The region immediately south of ancient Egypt.

pharaoh In the Old Kingdom the most common terms for the king were *hemef,* "His Majesty," or *nesw* "King." From the New Kingdom onward the term "pharaoh" was used, which came from the name of the palace, which was *per-aa* or "Great House."

Ramesseum Located in Luxor, Egypt, the memorial temple of Ramses II.

refugee A person who must leave his or her homeland due to a domestic or international emergency that destroys homes, threatens personal safety, or both.

sarcophagus An outer box that stored the mummified remains of a person.
Valley of the Kings New Kingdom royal necropolis located on the west bank of the Nile, about three miles west of modern Luxor.
vizier The vizier, or *tjaty*, was the chief minister of the government.

FOR MORE INFORMATION

American Research Center in Egypt (US Office)
8700 Crownhill Boulevard, Suite 507
San Antonio, TX 78209-1130
(210) 821-7000
Website: http://www.arce.org/main

This organization supports scholarship, training, and conservation efforts in Egypt and utilizes relationships with antiquities governance organizations.

Ancient Egypt Research Associates
26 Lincoln Street, Suite 5
Brighton, MA 02135
(617) 783-0737
Website: http://www.aeraweb.org

This far-reaching community backs research and supports education, conservation, and training to unveil the history and culture of ancient Egypt.

Archaeological Institute of America Headquarters
Boston University
656 Beacon Street, 6th Floor
Boston, MA 02215-2006
(617) 353-8708
Website: https://www.archaeological.org

This institute hosts lectures, workshops, and tours and creates records that share information on Egyptian cultural and natural heritage.

Canadian Museum of History
100 Laurier Street
Gatineau, QC K1A 0M8
Canada
(800) 555-5621
Website: http://www.historymuseum.ca
This museum hosts exhibitions, runs activities, and enables research in topics that include Egyptian history and archaeology.

Rosicrucian Egyptian Museum
1660 Park Avenue
San Jose, CA 95191
Website: http://www.egyptianmuseum.org
This museum hosts special events and a junior archaeologist training program for children and young adults, and its website also offers resources for education.

The Society for the Study of Egyptian Antiquities
PO Box 19004 Walmer
360A Bloor Street W

Toronto, ON M5S 3C9
Canada
(647) 520-4339
Website: http://www.thessea.org/index.php
This organization supports Egyptology studies and backs and promotes archaeological research in Egypt.

WEBSITES

Because of the changing nature of internet links, Rosen Publishing has developed an online list of websites related to the subject of this book. This site is updated regularly. Please use this link to access this list:

http://www.rosenlinks.com/LANW/ramsesii

Cline, Eric H. *1177 B.C.: The Year Civilization Collapsed* (Turning Points in Ancient History). Princeton, NJ: Princeton University Press, 2015.

Dodson, Aidan. *Amarna Sunrise: Egypt from Golden Age to Age of Heresy*. Cairo, Egypt: The American University in Cairo Press, 2014.

Garnett, Anna. *The Colossal Statue of Ramesses II* (Objects in Focus). London, UK: British Museum Press, 2015.

Goelet, Ogden (Translator), Raymond Faulkner (Translator), Carol Andrews (Preface), J. Daniel Gunther (Introduction), James Wasserman (Foreword). *The Egyptian Book of the Dead: The Book of Going Forth by Day: The Complete Papyrus of Ani Featuring Integrated Text and Full-Color Images*. San Francisco, CA: Chronicle Books, 2015.

Harari, Yuval Noah. *Sapiens: A Brief History of Humankind*. New York, NY: Harper, 2015.

Imhausen, Annette. *Mathematics in Ancient Egypt: A Contextual History*. Princeton, NJ: Princeton University Press, 2016.

Kuiper, Kathleen. *Ancient Egypt* (The Britannica Guide to Ancient Civilizations). New York, NY: Rosen Publishing, 2011.

Mears, Douglas. *Ramses and the Harem Conspiracy: The Nubian Physician*. Marina Del Rey, CA: Hauser Publishing, 2016.

Muhs, Brian. *The Ancient Egyptian Economy: 3000–30 BCE*. Cambridge, UK: Cambridge University Press, 2016.

Pemberton, Delia. *The Civilization of Ancient Egypt* (The Illustrated History of the Ancient World). New York, NY: Rosen Publishing, 2013.

Teeter, Emily. *Religion and Ritual in Ancient Egypt*. Cambridge, UK: Cambridge University Press, 2011.

Aldred, Cyril. *The Egyptians*. New York, NY: Thames & Hudson, 1998.

Baines, John, and Jaromir Malek. *Atlas of Ancient Egypt*. New York, NY: Facts on File, 1993.

Davies, Vivian, and Renee Friedman. *Egypt Uncovered*. New York, NY: Stewart, Tabori & Chang, 1998.

Bossone, Andrew. "Pharaoh Seti I's Tomb Bigger Than Thought." *National Geographic*, April 17, 2008. http://news.nationalgeographic.com/news/2008/04/080417-seti-tomb_2.html.

Franzen, Carl. "Ill-gotten Gains: How Many Museums Have Stolen Objects in Their Collections?" The Verge, May 13, 2013. http://www.theverge.com/2013/5/13/4326306/museum-artifacts-looted-repatriation.

Freed, Rita. *Ramses II: The Great Pharaoh and His Time*. Denver, CO: Denver Museum of Natural History, 1987.

Gabriel, Richard A., and Karen S. Metz. *A Short History of War: The Evolution of Warfare and Weapons*. Carlisle, PA: Strategic Studies Institute U.S. Army War College, 1992.

Hayes, William. *The Scepter of Egypt 2: The Hyksos Period and the New Kingdom*. New York, NY: Metropolitan Museum of Art, 1990.

Kitchen, Kenneth A. *Pharaoh Triumphant: The Life and Times of Ramesses II*. Warminster, UK: Aris and Phillips, 1982.

Quirke, Stephen. *Exploring Religion in Ancient Egypt*. New York, NY: Wiley, 2015.

Regents of the University of California. "Digital Karnak Timemap." 2008. http://dlib.etc.ucla.edu/projects/Karnak/timemap#

Shaw, Ian, and Paul Nicolson. *British Museum Dictionary of Ancient Egypt*. London, UK: British Museum Press, 1995.

Sheafer, Silvia Anne. *Ramses the Great* (Ancient World Leaders). New York, NY: Infobase Learning, 2013.

Snape, Steven. *Egyptian Temples*. Princes Risborough, UK: Shire, 1996.

University of Southern California. "History of Karnak." Retrieved October 7, 2016. http://www.usc.edu/dept/LAS/arc/karnak02/html/history.html.

Weiss, Tzivya S. "The Earliest Vehicles." Driving Change: Alternatively Fueled Vehicles (blog). Macaulay Honors College at CUNY, December 3, 2012. http://macaulay.cuny.edu/eportfolios/alternativevehicles/history/birth/.

ABOUT THE AUTHORS

Beatriz Santillian earned her BA in English in 2003, and her PhD in history in 2009. She is a fan of all things to do with ancient history and loves to learn about artifacts from the past. Santillian writes on topics to do with culture, technology, and change, and she also writes software in her spare time. She lives in Rochester, New York, with her daughter.

Susanna Thomas has a BA in Egyptian archaeology from University College, London, and was awarded a PhD from Liverpool University in 2000. She has worked sites all over Egypt, including in the Valley of the Kings, and runs excavations at Tell Abqa'in in the western Delta. She is particularly interested in vitreous materials and trade in the late Bronze Age.

PHOTO CREDITS

Cover, p. 3 Face_2_Face/Shutterstock.com; cover (background), pp. 6–7, 59 DEA/G. Dagli Orti/De Agostini/Getty Images; p. 13 DEA/S. Vannini/De Agostini/Getty Images; p. 16 Universal Images Group/Getty Images; pp. 18–19, 86–87 eFesenko/Shutterstock.com; p. 22 JSabel/iStock/Thinkstock; p. 25 Blaine Harrington III/Corbis Historical/Getty Images; p. 28 Tim E White/Cultura/Getty Images; pp. 32–33 De Agostini/G. Sioen/De Agostini Picture Library/Getty Images; pp. 38-39 Iberfoto/SuperStock; pp. 42–43 National Geographic Creative/Bridgeman Images; p. 46 Khaled Desouki/AFP/Getty Images; pp. 48–49 Quintanilla/Shutterstock.com; pp. 52–53, 96––97 Werner Forman/Universal Images Group/Getty Images; p. 55 © Tarker/Bridgeman Images; pp. 62–63 Philip and Elizabeth De Bay/Corbis Historical/Getty Images; p. 64 Universal Historical Archive/Universal Images Group/Getty Images; p. 70 Science & Society Picture Library/SSPL/Getty Images; p. 76 adoc-photos/Corbis Historical/Getty Images; p. 79 Brooklyn Museum of Art, New York, USA/Gift of Richard Abrams/Bridgeman Images; pp. 80–81 Ivy Close Images/Alamy Stock Photo; pp. 84–85 ScapeWare3d/DigitalGlobe/Getty Images; pp. 88–89 PHAS/Universal Images Group/Getty Images; interior pages background images © iStockphoto.com/kikkalek5050 (sky), Triff/Shutterstock.com (map).

Designer: Brian Garvey; Editor: Bernadette Davis; Photo Researcher: Karen Huang